Life As ...

Life As a Pony Express Rider in the Wild West

Matt Bougie

Cavendish Square
New York

Published in 2018 by Cavendish Square Publishing, LLC
243 5th Avenue, Suite 136, New York, NY 10016

First Edition

Website: cavendishsq.com

Library of Congress Cataloging-in-Publication Data

Names: Bougie, Matt, author.
Title: Life as a Pony Express rider in the Wild West / Matt Bougie.
Description: New York : Cavendish Square Publishing, 2018. |
Series: Life as ... | Includes bibliographical references and index.
Identifiers: LCCN 2017017144 (print) | LCCN 2017021727 (ebook) |
ISBN 9781502630506 (E-book) | ISBN 9781502630476 (paperback) |
ISBN 9781502630490 (library bound) | ISBN 9781502630483 (6 pack)
Subjects: LCSH: Pony express--Juvenile literature. | Horsemen and
horsewomen--West (U.S.)--History--19th century--Juvenile literature. |
Frontier and pioneer life--West (U.S.)--Juvenile literature. |
West (U.S.)--History--19th century--Juvenile literature.
Classification: LCC HE6375.P65 (ebook) | LCC HE6375.P65 B68 2018 (print) |
DDC 383/.1430973--dc23
LC record available at https://lccn.loc.gov/2017017144

Editorial Director: David McNamara
Editor: Kristen Susienka
Copy Editor: Rebecca Rohan
Associate Art Director: Amy Greenan
Designer: Lindsey Auten
Production Coordinator: Karol Szymczuk
Photo Research: J8 Media

The photographs in this book are used by permission and through the courtesy of: Cover, Print Collector/Hulton Archive/Getty Images; p. 5 Ed Vebell/Getty Images; p. 6 Education Images/UIG via Getty Images; p. 8 © Look and Learn/Bridgeman Images; p. 10 Peter Newark American Pictures/Bridgeman Images; p. 13 Pictorial Press Ltd/Alamy Stock Photo; p. 14 Hulton Archive/Getty Images; p. 16 Diane Garcia/Shutterstock.com; p. 18 Jkan997/Wikimedia Commons/File:Pony Express Route.svg; p. 20 Bettmann/Getty Images; p. 22 Michael E. Cumpston/Wikimedia Commons/File:Coltnewmodles.jpg; p. 23 Nat Farbman/The LIFE Picture Collection/Getty Images; p. 24 Ed Vebell/Getty Images; p. 26 CPret/Wikimedia Commons/File:Concord stagecoach 1869.png; p. 27 Everett Historical/Shutterstock.com.

Printed in the United States of America

Contents

Introduction	4
Chapter 1: A Speedy Solution	7
Chapter 2: Becoming a Rider	11
Chapter 3: A Day in the Life	17
Chapter 4: Tools of the Trade	21
Chapter 5: Becoming Part of History	25
Glossary	28
Find Out More	29
Index	32
About the Author	32

Introduction

Life in the United States in the early 1800s was hard, dangerous, and a lot of work. Many people were traveling to the West to seek new opportunities and to start a new life. People in the government or businesses in the East wanted to keep in contact with officials and business partners in the West.

While there were several services that would carry packages and letters by carriage, they were unreliable and slow. People living on the East Coast needed to send important messages west—specifically government orders, news, or business contracts—but there wasn't a reliable, fast service available. That is, until the Pony Express.

People gathered to see the novelty of the Pony Express riders, in addition to receiving the mail.

THE RISK TAKERS

This display at the National Pony Express Museum in St. Louis, Missouri, discusses the risks Russell, Majors, and Waddell took to start the mail service.

Chapter 1

A Speedy Solution

In the mid-1800s, the United States was expanding its territory. Many people wanted to start new lives or find gold in California and other areas on the Pacific coast. To do so, they had to travel across the country.

On September 9, 1850, California became a state. However, settlers had been living there for years. Mail delivery for businesses and government paperwork up to this point was unreliable and slow. It could take weeks for mail to get out to California, if it even arrived at all.

Even though the **telegraph** had been invented, it didn't reach all the way to California. Many other cities also did not have reliable means of communication. To communicate, people trusted others to carry their letters on horseback or by **stagecoach** across the wilderness.

There was no doubt a more organized system was needed. William Russell, Alexander Majors, and

Constructing the telegraph took a long time. The Pony Express delivered messages out west while people worked away.

William Waddell decided to do something about it. They created the Pony Express, a mail service that would carry important letters from Saint Joseph, Missouri, to Sacramento, California, and many other cities in between.

The Pony Express carried its first delivery westward on April 3, 1860.

High Expectations

The Pony Express was formed at a time when the United States was expanding westward at a rapid rate. By the 1850s, the founders of the Pony Express already had contracts with the US government to deliver supplies to the West. They thought that by offering very fast mail delivery, they could gain more contracts and expand their business. Unfortunately for Russell, Majors, and Waddell, these contracts never happened, and the Pony Express would not become a profitable or long-lasting enterprise.

Riders had to be tough enough to brave the harsh elements.

Chapter 2

Becoming a Rider

Pony Express riders were chosen carefully. To qualify, a young man had to be tough enough to ride miles and miles through the rough wilderness and also very light. Riders couldn't weigh more than 125 pounds (57 kilograms). This way, horses could run an entire stretch between **waypoints** without stopping.

If a young man met these qualifications, he could work for the Pony Express and make around three times what he could make working in town. With that kind of money at stake, many young men were eager to try their hand at this dangerous and challenging job.

Short but Sweet

The Pony Express only existed for eighteen months, from April 1860 to October 1861. However, in its short time, the company had eighty riders, more than one hundred stations, and between four hundred and five hundred horses.

By creating a **relay** system, a piece of mail could leave Saint Joseph, Missouri, and arrive in Sacramento, California, in nine days and twenty-three hours. That meant the letter traveled 250 miles (400 km) in twenty-four hours. Even though the road was dangerous and the conditions **hazardous**, the Pony Express only ever lost one shipment.

Not everyone could use the Pony Express, though. It was too expensive for citizens. The riders usually carried government documents and business contracts.

PONY EXPRESS!

CHANGE OF TIME!

REDUCED RATES!

10 Days to San Francisco!

LETTERS

WILL BE RECEIVED AT THE

OFFICE, 84 BROADWAY,

NEW YORK,

Up to 4 P. M. every TUESDAY,

AND

Up to 2½ P. M. every SATURDAY,

Which will be forwarded to connect with the PONY EXPRESS leaving ST. JOSEPH, Missouri,

Every WEDNESDAY and SATURDAY at 11 P. M.

TELEGRAMS

Sent to Fort Kearney on the mornings of MONDAY and FRIDAY, will connect with **PONY** leaving St. Joseph, WEDNESDAYS and SATURDAYS.

EXPRESS CHARGES.

LETTERS weighing half ounce or under..............$1 00
For every additional half ounce or fraction of an ounce 1 CO
In all cases to be enclosed in 10 cent Government Stamped Envelopes,

And all Express CHARGES Pre-paid.

☞ **PONY EXPRESS ENVELOPES For Sale at our Office.**

WELLS, FARGO & CO., Ag'ts.

New York, July 1, 1861.

SLOTE & JANES, STATIONERS AND PRINTERS, 93 FULTON STREET, NEW YORK

This poster explains how the Pony Express worked.

Buffalo Bill Cody circa 1885

Riders and Legends

Pony Express riders could be young boys and grown men. One man named "Bronco" Charlie Miller claimed he was eleven years old when he became a rider. Other people convinced people they were riders, even though they never officially rode for the Pony Express. One of these legends was William F. "Buffalo Bill" Cody. Cody claimed he became a rider at the age of fourteen. He might have worked for the owners of the company, but he probably never was a Pony Express rider. Still, as an adult, he helped people remember the Pony Express in his Wild West shows.

Small stations along the way allowed a rider to change his horse and resupply.

Chapter 3

A Day in the Life

Being a Pony Express rider was a challenging job. Riders would travel around 75 miles (121 km) per day. This took them over rocky roads and steep hills. They would travel in any kind of weather. Riders met snow, rain, storms, and sunshine on their journeys.

Horses also worked hard. They had to travel 10 to 15 miles (16 to 24 km) in one day. They also had to be sure not to trip and fall or break a leg. If that happened, the rider needed to abandon the horse and continue on foot, sprinting to the next post. After all, making the delivery on time was the key selling point of the Pony Express.

Besides weather, Pony Express riders met Native Americans on their way. In the 1800s, the American government and the military pushed Native

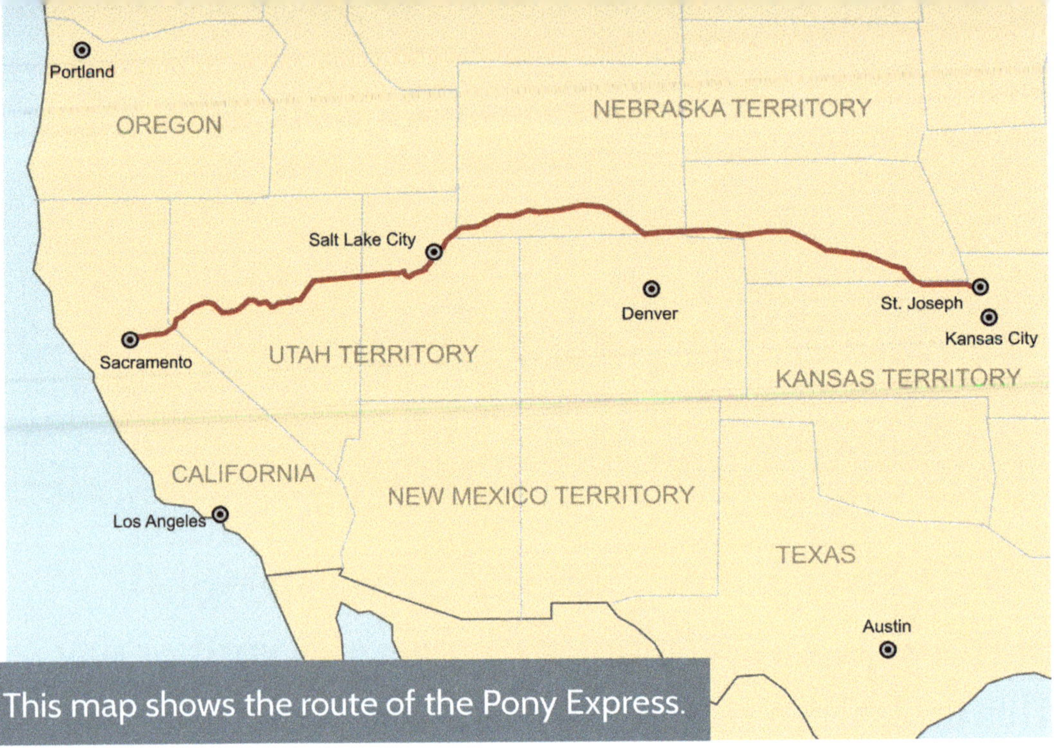

This map shows the route of the Pony Express.

Americans off their land and destroyed their homes. Many Native people were angry. They would attack travelers. A Pony Express rider was an attractive target.

The people at the Pony Express stations also experienced danger. Stations, called outposts, were **static** targets with valuable items nearby and inside. They also weren't **fortified** well. Groups of Native Americans would attack these stations and steal goods.

During the operation of the Pony Express, stations were burned down and horses were stolen or driven off. Several riders and station workers even lost their lives.

A Rider's Schedule

The Pony Express prided itself on fast and reliable delivery. Because the mail never stopped moving, a rider's day could start at nine in the morning or nine at night—or anytime in between! This schedule gives you an idea of what a rider's day (or night) might be like.

Step One:	Leave station after resting and eating a hot meal.
Step Two:	Ride a fresh horse for 10 to 15 miles (16 to 24 km).
Step Three:	Reach the next station and exchange horses.
Step Four:	Repeat steps two and three until you've ridden 75 miles (121 km).
Step Five:	Exchange riders and horses and repeat steps two to four.
Step Six:	Last rider reaches his final destination.

This painting shows a Pony Express rider leaving a waypoint.

Chapter 4

Tools of the Trade

Pony Express riders had a few tools that they always carried. The number of tools changed over time, though. This helped the riders reach their checkpoints faster.

Pony Express riders wanted to be able to stop as few times as possible along the route. They also wanted to be able to protect themselves if needed. However, the more that a rider carried, the slower the horse would run. This is why riders limited what they carried, leaving almost all comfort items at home. By the time the Pony Express ended in 1861, riders carried nothing but the mail, the Bible, a water sack, and a pistol.

Not only did Pony Express riders limit their supplies, but they looked to lighten the load in any way they could. For example, they worked to make the seat in which they sat lighter. Special saddles were invented for this purpose. Called mochillas, they had four locked pockets made out of heavy leather that could hold belongings.

These special saddles had another important feature that was vital to Pony Express riders. Because

The Colt revolver was a rugged weapon for everyone in the Wild West.

The Colt Revolver

Pistols were important for a rider to carry because they were the only way that he could defend himself from attacks. If a rider was attacked on the road, he was expected to do all he could to ensure that the mail got delivered.

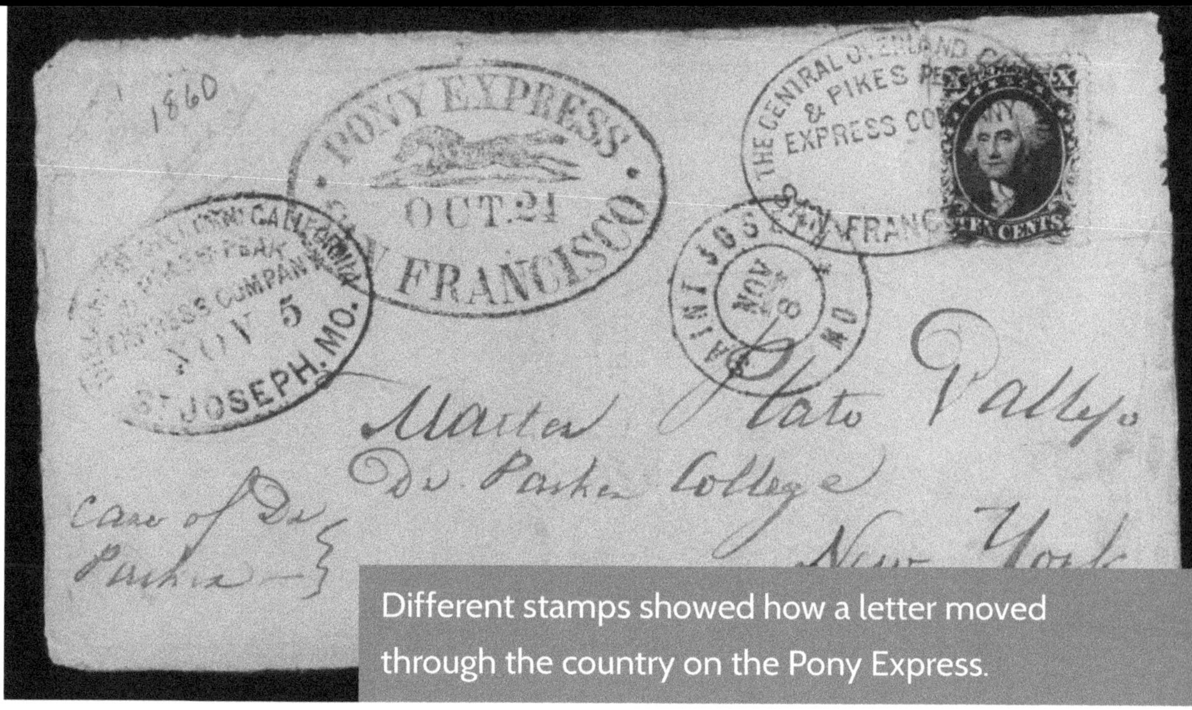

Different stamps showed how a letter moved through the country on the Pony Express.

riders changed horses eight to ten times before their day was done, it was very important to make those transitions *fast*. Mochillas allowed a rider to jump off of a tired horse, grab all of the cargo, sling it onto a fresh horse, and take off again—all in under two minutes! By speeding up these transitions, riders shaved hours off the journey.

The most important tool a rider carried was the mail. After all, these letters and packages made the Pony Express possible. Each piece would be carefully stamped along the way, telling the person receiving the mail that it had come by way of the Pony Express.

This painting shows a Pony Express rider being followed by Native Americans.

Chapter 5

Becoming Part of History

The Pony Express operated for eighteen months. In that time, the riders delivered around thirty-five thousand pieces of mail. When a telegraph system linking the East Coast and the West Coast was completed in 1861, there became little need for the expensive, high-speed mail delivery system. Packages and letters were still carried by stagecoaches, since those services were more affordable for everyday people.

On October 26, 1861, two days after the telegraph lines were completed, the Pony Express announced that they were closing. Final deliveries were made in November, and the Pony Express became a part of history. However, it would live on for a time through

After the Pony Express closed, stagecoaches were still used to carry mail and packages across the country.

Buffalo Bill's Wild West shows, with fast horse changes and other fancy riding techniques.

There is some debate on why the Pony Express closed so quickly. Some say that the owners had an agreement to stop once the telegraph lines were completed. Others say that they were losing lots of money and the completion of the telegraph lines was the final straw.

The Pony Express didn't last long, but it made an impact on American culture that still exists today. Much of how we think about the Wild West—with horse riders, frontiersmen, and the free spirit of the West—comes from the riders of the Pony Express.

The Pony Express will always be an iconic image of the Wild West.

Glossary

fortified Strengthened in defense to protect against an attack.

hazardous Dangerous or risky.

relay A system where a person travels from one point to another and hands materials off to someone else to continue the journey.

stagecoach A horse-drawn carriage used to carry mail.

static Lacking in movement, fixed and constant.

telegraph A device that allowed electrical signals to be transferred through wires, allowing for the transmission of messages quickly across long distances.

waypoint A stopping point, or a resting place on a long journey.

Find Out More

Books

Landsborough, Gordon. *Riders of the Pony Express*. London, UK: Pioneering Press, 2017.

Ratliff, Tom, and Mark Bergin. *You Wouldn't Want to Be a Pony Express Rider!* New York: Scholastic, 2012.

Warren, Louis S. *Buffalo Bill's America: William Cody and the Wild West Show*. New York: Alfred A. Knopf, 2005.

Website

History Lists: Ten Things You May Not Know About the Pony Express

http://www.history.com/news/history-lists/10-things-you-may-not-know-about-the-pony-express

Video

Today I Found Out: The Surprisingly Short History of the Pony Express

https://www.youtube.com/watch?v=3vrzi-BEjWs

Index

Page numbers in **boldface** are illustrations. Entries in **boldface** are glossary terms.

Cody, Buffalo Bill, **14, 15, 26**

fortified, 18

hazardous, 12

Majors, Alexander, **6, 8–9**
mochillas, 5, 22–23, 24

Native Americans, 17–18, 24

relay, 12
riders, **5, 10, 11–12, 15, 17–19, 20, 21–23, 24, 25–26, 27**
route, 18
Russell, William, 6, 8–9

Sacramento, California, 9, 12
Saint Joseph, Missouri, 9, 12
schedule, 19

stagecoach, 8, 25, **26**
static, 18

telegraph, 7, **8, 25–26**

Waddell, William, 6, 9
waypoint, 11, **16**

About the Author

Matt Bougie grew up in a small town in central Wisconsin. After graduating from St. Norbert College in De Pere, Wisconsin, he moved to Milwaukee, Wisconsin, to pursue a career. He still lives there with his girlfriend Dani and their two dogs. He works at a marketing company and as a freelance writer. In his free time, he enjoys watching sports, riding his bicycle, and reading.